neighborhoods in nature™

Let's Take a Field Trip to the Deep Sea

Kathy Furgang

The Rosen Publishing Group's
PowerKids Press™
New York

✹ For Sam and Sandy ✹

Special thanks to the Woods Hole Oceanographic Institution

Published in 2000 by The Rosen Publishing Group, Inc.
29 East 21st Street, New York, NY 10010

Copyright © 2000 by The Rosen Publishing Group, Inc.

Photo Credits: p. 4 © Wayne Green, © Animals, Animals/Rudolf Ingo Riepl, © Woods Hole Oceanographic Institution; p. 5 © Wayne Green, © Christopher Swaan/Peter Arnold, Inc.; p. 7 © Woods Hole Oceanographic Institution; p. 8 © Animals, Animals/Randy Morse, © Animals, Animals/Chuck Wise, © Animals, Animals/R. Kuiter, O.S.F., © Norbert Wu/Peter Arnold, Inc., © Norbert Wu/Peter Arnold, Inc.; p. 9 © Norbert Wu/Peter Arnold, Inc.; p. 10 © Animals, Animals/O.S.F.; p. 11 © Animals, Animals/O.S.F., © Animals, Animals/P. Parks, O.S.F., © Norbert Wu/Peter Arnold, Inc.; p. 12 © Woods Hole Oceanographic Institution; p. 13 © Doug Perrine/Peter Arnold, Inc.; pp. 14, 15 © CORBIS; p. 16 © Earth Scenes/Breck P. Kent, © Woods Hole Oceanographic Institution; p. 17 © Christopher Swaan/Peter Arnold, Inc.; pp. 19, 20 © Woods Hole Oceanographic Institution; p. 21 © FPG/Telegraph Colour Library; p. 22 © NASA/Peter Arnold,Inc.; p. 23 © Woods Hole Oceanographic Institution.

Photo Illustrations by Thaddeus Harden

First Edition

Book Design: Felicity Erwin

Furgang, Kathy.
    Let's take a field trip to the deep sea / by Kathy Furgang.
        p.   cm. — (Neighborhoods in nature)
    Includes index.
    Summary: Describes the deepest layer of the ocean including its floor, water pressure, darkness, temperatures, unique animals and their food, and the work of oceanographers in submersibles.
    ISBN 0-8239-5448-X (lib. bdg.)
    1. Deep-sea ecology Juvenile literature. [1. Marine ecology. 2. Ecology.] I. Title. II. Series: Furgang, Kathy. Neighborhoods in nature.
QH541.5.D35F87 1999
577.7'7—dc21
                                                                                99-18065
                                                                                CIP

Manufactured in the United States of America

Contents

1	Layers of the Ocean	5
2	The Ocean Floor	6
3	Life in the Deep Sea	9
4	Fish That Light Up	10
5	Survival in the Deep	13
6	Finding Food in the Deep	14
7	Exploring the Ocean Floor	17
8	Harsh Conditions	18
9	Earthquake!	21
10	Scientists and the Deep Sea	22
	Web Sites	22
	Glossary	23
	Index	24

photic

twilight

abyssal

Layers of the Ocean

There's much more to the ocean than what we can see from the beach. The ocean covers 71 percent of Earth's surface. Parts of the ocean reach many miles below the surface. The ocean is made up of three layers. The **photic** layer is closest to the surface. It goes down a couple hundred feet. People swim in the photic layer. The middle layer is called the **twilight** layer. It is darker because less light can reach it. The **abyssal** layer is the deepest. It is miles below the surface of the sea where there is no sunlight at all.

The deep sea is a world that is almost totally untouched by people. We cannot visit the deep sea, even for a short time, without the help of machines.

The Ocean Floor

There are mountains on the ocean floor. Some of them reach miles high. Sometimes these mountains are so tall that they reach the surface of the ocean and form islands. That means islands are just the tops of underwater mountains. The bottom of the sea is also full of **volcanoes**. A volcano is an opening in the surface of Earth that shoots up a hot liquid rock, called **lava**. In addition to mountains and volcanoes, the ocean floor has deep cracks called **trenches**. These ocean trenches stretch as far down into the ocean floor as the highest mountains stretch up towards the sky.

The ocean floor is as old as our planet. Some trenches, mountains, and volcanoes ▶
hidden deep beneath the sea have been around for millions of years.

An underwater landscape

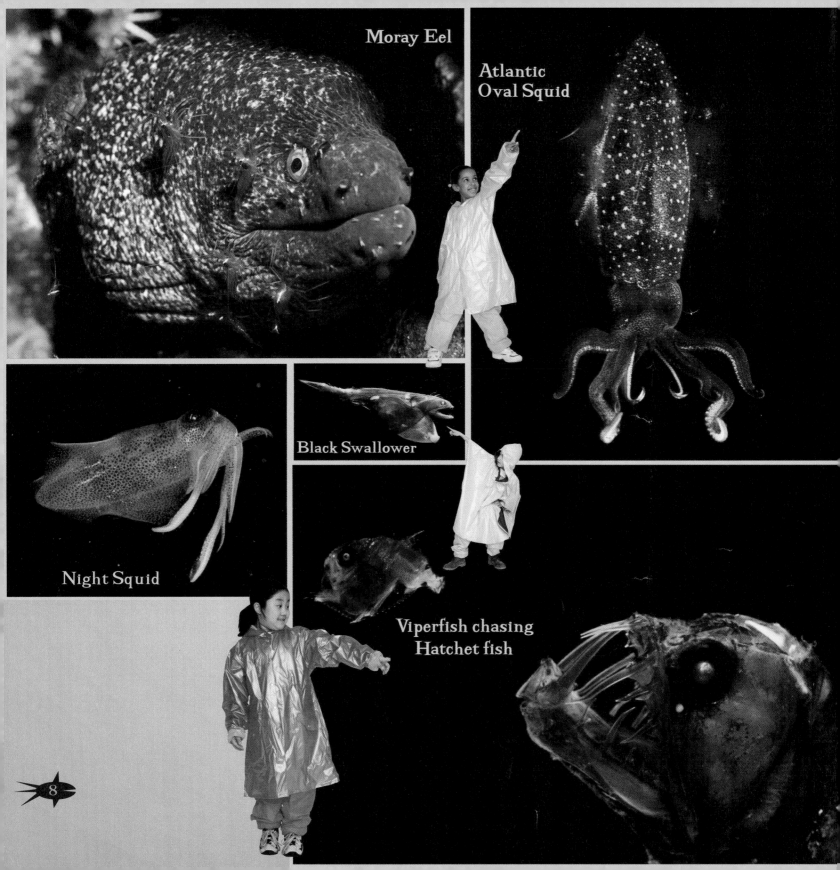

Moray Eel

Atlantic
Oval Squid

Black Swallower

Night Squid

Viperfish chasing
Hatchet fish

8

Life in the Deep Sea

Deep Sea Toad

If you've ever wondered what it would be like to live in the deep sea, imagine total darkness. Then imagine feeling some areas of freezing cold water around you. As you swim along, boiling lava from volcanoes make some areas of water very hot. You can go from cold to hot water in a second and then back to cold water again. Life on the ocean bottom can be hard for the **communities** of fish that live there. It is easy for these underwater creatures to be killed from the heat of volcanoes and the movement of dangerous **earthquakes** on the ocean floor. Squids, viperfish, and eels all live in the deep sea.

◀ *These fish that live in the deep sea use long, sharp teeth to find food.*

Fish That Light Up

The deep sea can sometimes look like a night sky that is filled with the flash of lightning bugs. Since there is no light on the ocean floor, many fish have their own lights—on their bodies! When a creature makes its own light, it is called **bioluminescence**. These fish light up only when they want to. They shine so that they can see better in the dark and catch food. When they see their **prey**, they blind it with their bright light to slow it down. Then they catch and eat their prey. If a bioluminescent fish senses danger, it can turn off its light to hide from its enemies.

These bioluminescent fish are found only in the deep sea and can live from 1,000–3,000 feet below the surface of the ocean. ▶

Hatchet Fish

Comb Jellyfish

Red Comb Jellyfish

11

Survival
in the Deep

Sperm Whale

Humans cannot survive for even one minute in the deep sea because the water **pressure**, or weight, is much too high. In the deepest part of the ocean, the pressure can be greater than eight tons. This weight is equal to one person trying to hold up 50 jumbo jets! Bioluminescent fish can live in the deep sea, but they would not be able to live on land. The pressure on land would be too low for them to survive. Some animals, such as the sperm whale, do not live in the deep sea, but they swim there to find food and then return to their homes in the twilight layer of the ocean.

Some sea animals survive by eating bacteria. Giant tube worms up to 12 feet long cling to the sides of volcanoes. One end of the worm attaches to the ground, and the other end eats bacteria from the seawater.

Finding Food in the Deep

Deep Sea Urchins

There is a lot of good food hidden in the mud on the ocean floor. Tiny pieces of food float around in the ocean. Also, when a fish eats, pieces of food fall from its mouth to the ocean floor. The food pieces settle in the mud and are eaten later by other sea animals. A lot of food falls down from the twilight layer too. Dead sea creatures sometimes sink down from this ocean layer and settle on the sea floor.

Although fish often catch and eat sea creatures whole, they can always snack on the leftover goodies that have settled on the ocean floor. ▶

Crocodile Fish

Blue Spotted Stingray

15

Research mini-sub

Alvin

Exploring the Ocean Floor

Scientists have invented special machines called **submersibles** that help us visit the deep dark sea. Scientists travel inside of submersibles to learn more about the deep sea. These machines are made so that people can safely travel to where the water pressure is very high. Scientists can look out windows to observe the amazing creatures that live near the ocean floor. Creatures are collected through special tubes so that they can be studied. **Alvin** is the name of a well-known submersible that carries three people at a time to the deep sea. Since the water pressure in the deep sea is too high for the scientists to swim in, the scientists have robots they can send out to take pictures of the ocean floor.

◀ *Alvin, a submersible from the Woods Hole Oceanographic Institution, has found gold, silver, and copper on the ocean floor.*

Harsh Conditions

Deep-sea exploration has taught us a lot about the ocean floor. Submersibles keep track of water temperatures. As you go farther and farther down into the ocean, the water becomes colder and colder. No light can reach the ocean floor, so the water can never warm up from the sun. Even though most of the water in the deep sea is icy and near freezing, the water near deep-sea volcanoes reaches deathly hot temperatures. Hot lava comes out of volcanoes like fire and heats the areas of water around it to about 700 degrees.

The lava from these volcanoes comes from the center of Earth. ▶
The ocean floor is as close as we can get to Earth's center.

Earthquake!

An earthquake is a strong shaking or violent movement of the ground. Earthquakes that happen on land can cause severe damage to the surrounding areas. An earthquake happens when underground rock moves or when volcanoes **erupt**, or explode, and cause rocks to move. We do not feel many earthquakes because they often happen on the ocean floor. Earthquakes under the water make very large waves. Some of these earthquakes are so strong that they cause giant waves that travel across the ocean and in time, hit the land. These dangerous waves are called **tsunamis**.

◀ *When earthquakes happen on the sea floor, dirt and sand make the ocean water very muddy.*

Scientists and the Deep Sea

Scientists are slowly figuring out the many mysteries of the deep sea. Scientists who study the ocean and sea creatures are called **oceanographers**. They have discovered that the ocean floor is a lot like the surface of other planets, such as Jupiter. Volcanoes and rocky surfaces are found in both places. Scientists are working hard to learn more and more about the deep sea. There are still many exciting areas of the ocean to be discovered.

Web Sites

To learn more about the ocean and the deep sea, visit these Web sites:

http://www.seasky.org/sea5a.html

http://seawifs.gsfc.nasa.gov/squid.html

http://www.extremescience.com/DeepestFish.htm

http://geosun1.sjsu.edu/~dreed/onset/exer3/exploring.html

Glossary

abyssal (uh-BIH-sul) The deepest layer of the ocean where no light reaches.

Alvin (AL-vin) The nickname of a particular submersible used to explore the ocean floor.

bioluminescence (BY-oh-loo-mih-NEH-sens) When a creature is able to make its own light.

communities (kuh-MYOO-nih-teez) Groups of people or animals that share things in common and help to care for one another.

earthquakes (URTH-kwayks) When the crust of Earth shakes as a result of two plates running into one another.

erupt (ih-RUPT) To explode.

lava (LAH-vuh) Hot liquid made of melted rock that comes out of a volcano.

oceanographer (oh-shin-AH-gruh-fur) A scientist who studies the ocean.

photic (FO-tik) The top layer of the ocean that gets light from the sun.

pressure (PREH-shur) A force that pushes on something.

prey (PRAY) An animal that is eaten by another animal for food.

submersible (sub-MUR-sih-bul) A machine that allows scientists to study the ocean.

trenches (TRENCH-ez) Deep cracks in the ocean floor.

tsunamis (soo-NAM-eez) Waves caused by a disturbance in Earth's crust under or near the ocean.

twilight (TWY-lyt) The middle layer of the ocean. It receives very little light from the sun.

volcanoes (vol-KAY-noz) Openings in the surface of Earth that sometimes shoot up a hot liquid rock called lava.

Index

A
abyssal, 5
Alvin, 17

B
beach, 5
bioluminescence, 10,
    13

C
communities, 9

E
earthquakes, 9, 21
eel, 9
erupt, 21
exploration, 18

F
fish, 9, 10, 13, 14
food, 14

I
islands, 6

L
lava, 6, 9, 18

M
mountains, 6

O
ocean floor, 6, 10,
    14, 17, 18, 22
oceanographers, 22

P
photic, 5
pressure, 13, 17
prey, 10

S
scientists, 17, 22
sperm whale, 13
squids, 9

submersibles, 17, 18
sunlight, 5

T
temperature, 9, 18
trenches, 6
tsunamis, 21
twilight, 5, 13, 14

V
viperfish, 9
volcanoes, 6, 9, 18,
    21, 22

AAW-6038